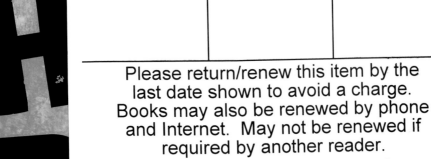

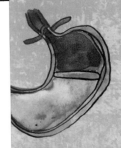

Anna Claybourne

Illustrated by Chrissy Barnard

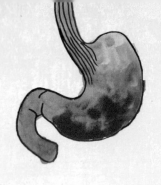

First published in paperback in 2016 by Wayland

Dewey number: 612–dc23
ISBN: 978 0 7502 8972 6
Library ebook ISBN: 978 0 7502 8831 6
10 9 8 7 6 5 4 3 2 1

MIX
Paper from responsible sources
FSC® C104740
FSC www.fsc.org

Series editor: Victoria Brooker
Series design: Lisa Peacock

A CIP catalogue record for this book is available
from the British Library.

Wayland is an imprint of Hachette Children's Group
Part of Hodder & Stoughton
Carmelite House
50 Victoria Embankment
London EC4Y 0DZ

Printed in China

An Hachette UK Company
www.hachette.co.uk
www.hachettechildrens.co.uk

Contents

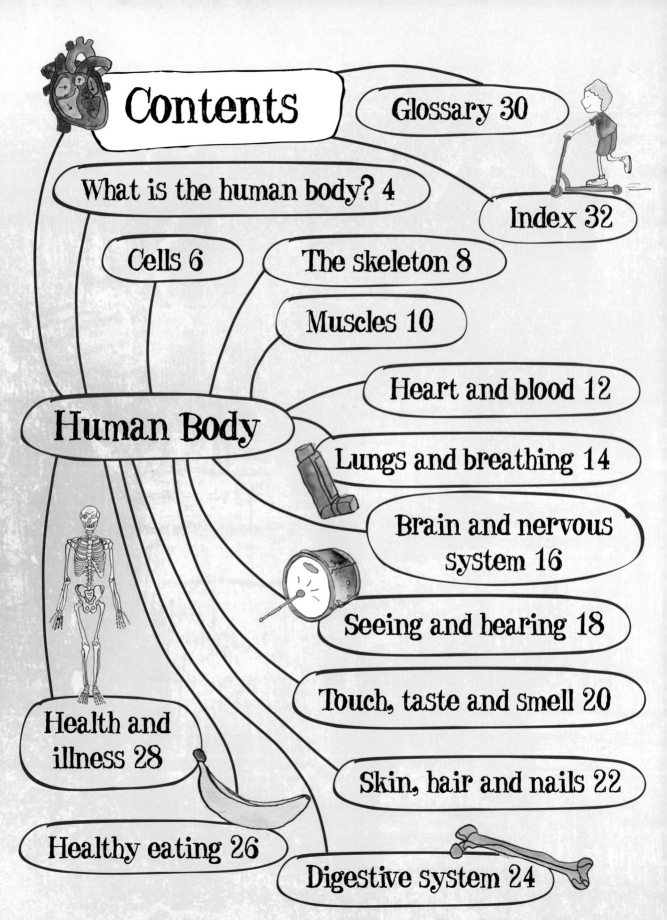

What is the human body?

You live in an amazing machine. It walks and runs, talks and sings, thinks and grows, takes in food and oxygen, and gets rid of the waste it doesn't need. It fights germs, keeps itself cool or warm, and if it gets cut or scratched, it can heal itself! In fact, it can even make new copies of itself. It's the human body – an incredibly complex and clever living thing.

Built from bits

Like other living things, the human body is made up of tiny units called cells. Most of them are far too small to see on their own. But together, they form larger body parts, such as bones, muscles, skin and blood, and organs like the brain, stomach and heart. The human body, and the cells it is made of, also contain a lot of water. A typical human is about 60% water.

Body parts also work together in groups, to form body systems. Each body system does a particular job for the body. For example, the digestive system takes food into the body and breaks it down into chemicals for the body to use. The digestive system includes the mouth, stomach and intestines. The circulatory system carries blood around the body. It includes the heart and blood vessels. This book explores the body's main systems, the organs they are made of, and how they work.

What is a mind web?

In this book, all the facts you need to know about the human body are arranged into mind webs. A mind web is a way of laying out information about a topic on a single page. The topic title goes in the middle, with all the important facts and words arranged around it. There are lines to link things together, and little pictures to help you remember things.

Mind webs are very useful for helping you think, learn and sort out ideas. They let you see a topic all at once, showing how all the parts are linked together. Because the mind web looks like a picture, your brain may also find it easier to remember. Mind webs can also be called mind maps, spidergrams or spider graphs. This mini mind web shows some of the main topics to do with the human body.

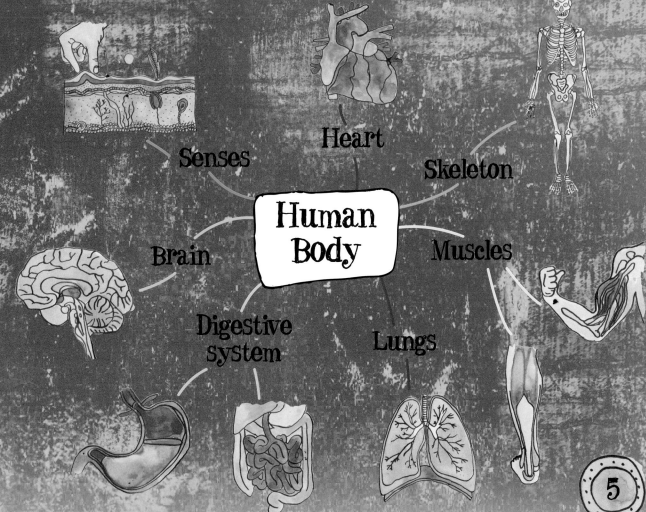

Senses

Heart

Skeleton

Brain

Human Body

Muscles

Digestive system

Lungs

control how
cells work

spiral-
shaped
chemical

found in
cell nucleus

give instructions
to cells

DNA

sections of DNA

genes

**Genes and
DNA**

stomach

brain

eye

heart

organs

make body
parts

50-100 trillion
in 1 human body

Human cells

Cells

liver

liver cells

brain

**Types of
human cells**

rod and
cone cells

nerves

neurons

muscle
cells

red blood
cells

white
blood cells

sense light
in the eye

skin
cells

muscle

blood

blood

fight germs

skin

carry oxygen

6

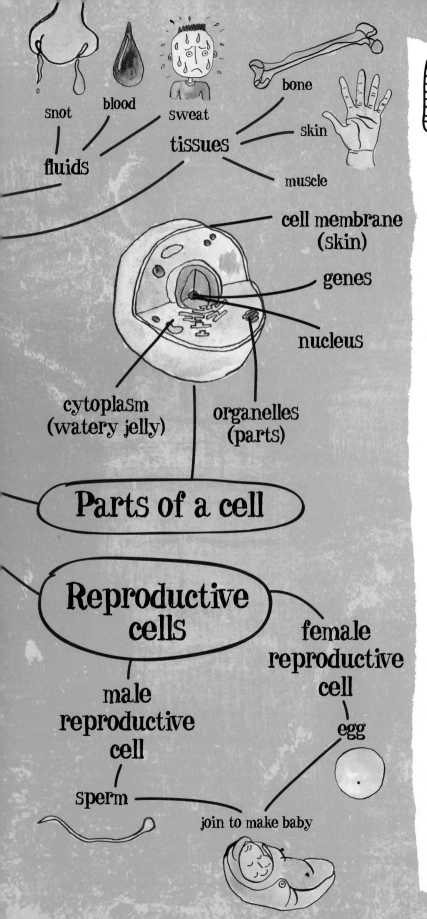

snot

blood

sweat

bone

skin

muscle

tissues

fluids

cell membrane (skin)

genes

nucleus

cytoplasm (watery jelly)

organelles (parts)

Parts of a cell

Reproductive cells

female reproductive cell

male reproductive cell

egg

sperm

join to make baby

Cells

Cells are the tiny parts that make up living things. They work together in groups to form all the different body parts and to keep the body working. Each cell has its own skin or cell membrane, and its own tiny parts, or organelles. Most cells have a nucleus, or control centre, containing genes. These are instructions that tell cells what to do, and control the way the body works and grows. Slight differences in genes make humans different from each other.

Human cells
The body has about 200 types of cell. For example, muscles are made of muscle cells and the brain and nerves are made of special nerve cells, or neurons. Altogether, a typical, fully grown human body is made up of around 50–100 trillion cells!

Reproduction
The human body also contains reproductive cells, whose job is to make new human beings. When male and female reproductive cells join together, they make a new cell that can grow into a baby.

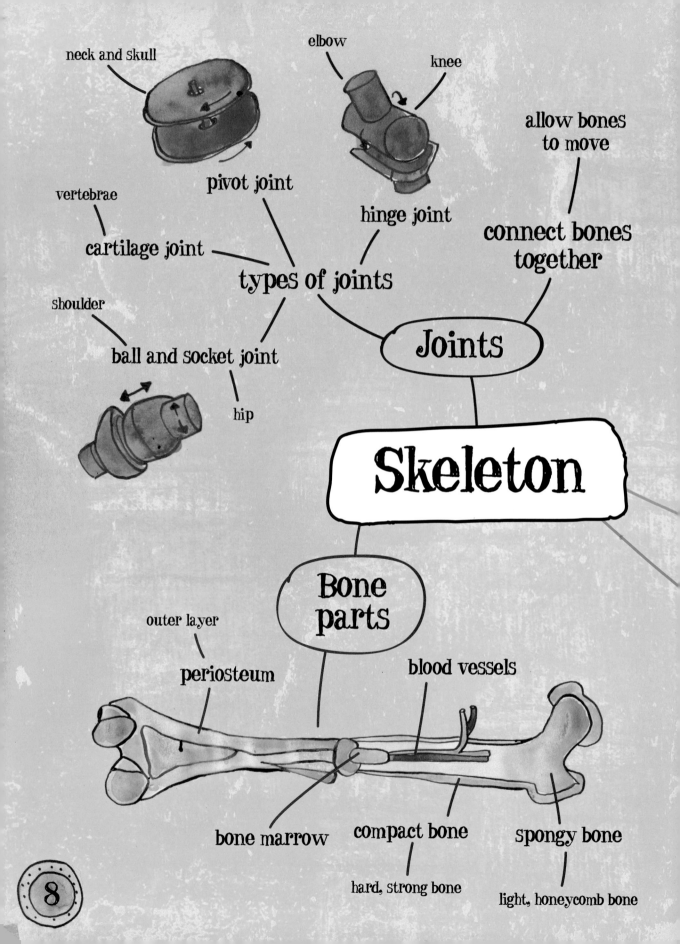

neck and skull

elbow

knee

pivot joint

vertebrae

hinge joint

allow bones
to move

cartilage joint

types of joints

connect bones
together

shoulder

ball and socket joint

Joints

hip

Skeleton

Bone
parts

outer layer

blood vessels

periosteum

bone marrow

compact bone

spongy bone

hard, strong bone

light, honeycomb bone

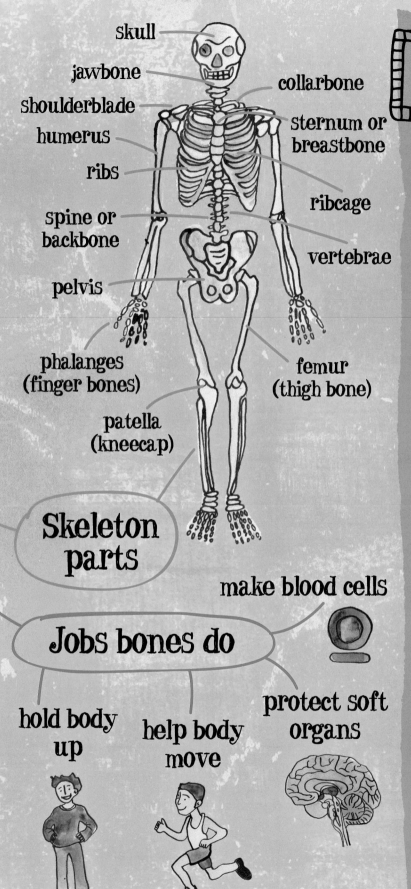

skull

jawbone

shoulderblade

humerus

ribs

spine or
backbone

pelvis

phalanges
(finger bones)

patella
(kneecap)

collarbone

sternum or
breastbone

ribcage

vertebrae

femur
(thigh bone)

Skeleton parts

Jobs bones do

make blood cells

hold body up

help body move

protect soft organs

The skeleton

The skeleton is the framework inside your body, made up of more than 200 different bones. Your skeleton has several jobs to do. It holds your body up and gives it its shape. Parts of your skeleton, such as the skull and the ribcage, protect soft but important organs, like the brain, heart and lungs. Bones are connected together by moving joints. This means that bones can work with muscles to move your body into different positions. Bones also have another important job — they make blood cells and release them into the blood.

Inside a bone
Bones are hard, but they are not solid or dead. A typical bone has a hard outer layer or periosteum, with a layer of hard or compact bone underneath it. Inside this is lighter spongy bone that looks like a honeycomb. Large bones also contain a soft fatty substance called bone marrow, where blood cells are made.

Muscles

Muscles are a type of body tissue that your body uses to move. There are muscles all over your skeleton, attached to your bones with strong, stretchy strings called tendons. They are called skeletal muscles and you have more than 600 of them. There is also lots more muscle inside your body, known as smooth muscle. It makes organs and other body parts do the movements that make them work. For example, smooth muscle in your stomach makes it squeeze and squish food to mush it up. The heart also has to squeeze to pump blood. It's made of a special type of muscle called cardiac muscle.

Pulling

Muscles work by getting shorter, or contracting, and pulling on other body parts. Muscles can't push – they can only pull, then relax. So to move a body part such as the elbow, there are often two muscles working together. One pulls to move the elbow one way, and another pulls to move it back the other way.

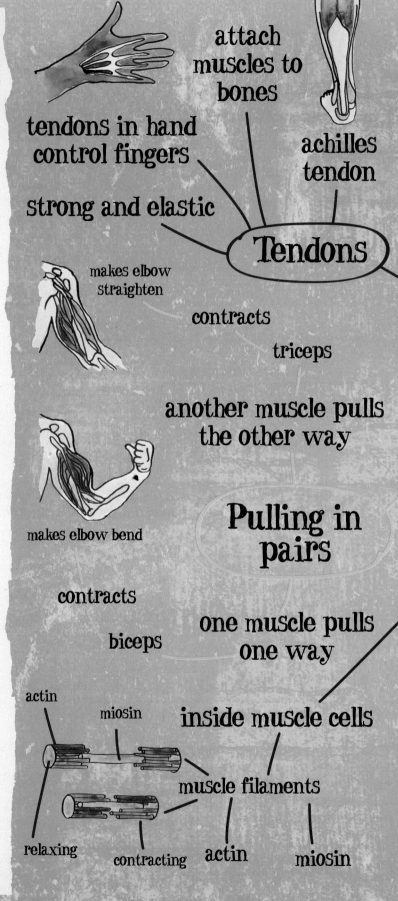

attach muscles to bones

tendons in hand control fingers

strong and elastic

achilles tendon

Tendons

makes elbow straighten

contracts

triceps

another muscle pulls the other way

makes elbow bend

Pulling in pairs

contracts

biceps

one muscle pulls one way

actin

miosin

inside muscle cells

muscle filaments

relaxing

contracting

actin

miosin

attached to bones

skeletal muscles

in organs and body parts

smooth muscles

in the heart

cardiac muscles

Types of muscle

Muscles

Main muscles

How muscles pull

contracting

muscle gets shorter and pulls

relaxing

muscle gets longer

pectoral

deltoid

trapezius

biceps

triceps

abdominal

quadriceps

gluteal

calf muscles

FRONT

BACK

watery yellow liquid

blood is 80% water

lead away from heart

lead back to heart

smallest blood vessels

arteries

veins

capillaries

tubes that carry blood

Blood vessels

plasma

red blood cells

Blood parts

Heart and blood

carry oxygen

platelets

white blood cells

repair cuts and injuries

fight germs

medicines

Jobs blood does

oxygen

delivers

food chemicals

takes away waste chemicals

fights germs and heals cuts

water

hormones

signalling chemicals

spreads warmth around body

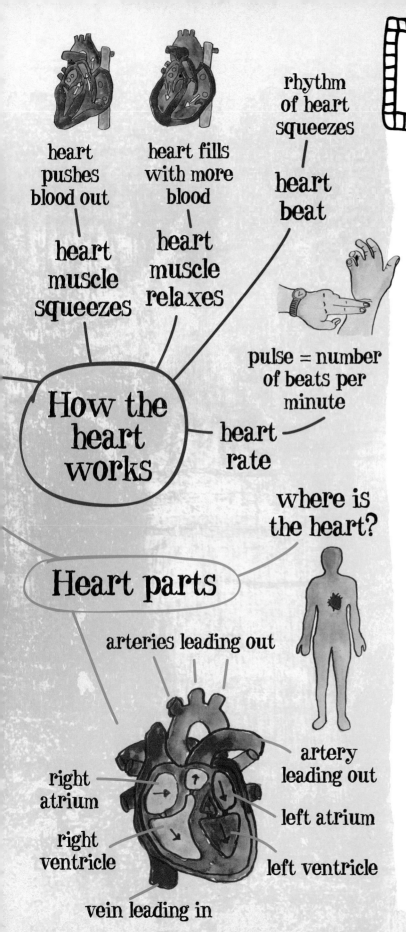

heart pushes blood out

heart fills with more blood

heart muscle squeezes

heart muscle relaxes

rhythm of heart squeezes

heart beat

How the heart works

pulse = number of beats per minute

heart rate

where is the heart?

Heart parts

arteries leading out

right atrium

right ventricle

artery leading out

left atrium

left ventricle

vein leading in

Your heart keeps working 24 hours a day, all your life. Its job is to pump blood around the body by squeezing tightly. Blood can pass through the heart in one direction only, so each time it squeezes, it pushes a bit more blood on its way around the body.

What is blood for?

Blood delivers oxygen gas to all the body's cells. Cells need a constant supply of oxygen to turn fuel into energy. Without this oxygen, muscles would stop working, and you would not be able to breathe or move. Blood collects oxygen as it flows through the lungs, then carries it to the rest of the body. Blood also carries other useful things around the body, including water, food, medicines and hormones.

Blood vessels

The heart is connected to a huge network of blood vessels that lead to all parts of the body. Vessels leading away from the heart are called arteries, and those that lead back to the heart are called veins.

13

Lungs and breathing

The lungs are two big, spongy organs inside your chest. They suck air into your body, extract oxygen from it and put the oxygen into your blood so that it can be delivered to all the body's cells. At the same time, the lungs collect a waste gas that the body makes, carbon dioxide, and breathe it back out. Inside the lungs, there are lots of branching passageways, leading to tiny chambers called alveoli. The alveoli are surrounded by billions of even smaller blood vessels. As you breathe in, air fills the alveoli, and the gases move into and out of the blood vessels through their walls.

Breathing bits

You breathe in and out through your nose and mouth. They are connected to the trachea or windpipe, a tube that leads to the lungs. To breathe in, muscles in your chest and under your lungs pull your lungs open, sucking air inside. To breathe out, the muscles squeeze the lungs and push air out again.

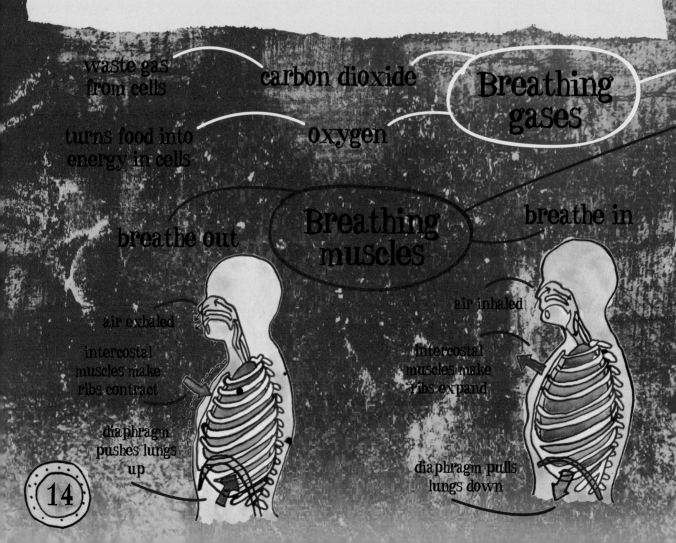

waste gas from cells

carbon dioxide

Breathing gases

turns food into energy in cells

oxygen

breathe out

Breathing muscles

breathe in

air exhaled

air inhaled

intercostal muscles make ribs contract

intercostal muscles make ribs expand

diaphragm pushes lungs up

diaphragm pulls lungs down

breathing in

extract
oxygen
into blood

breathing out

collect
carbon
dioxide
out of blood

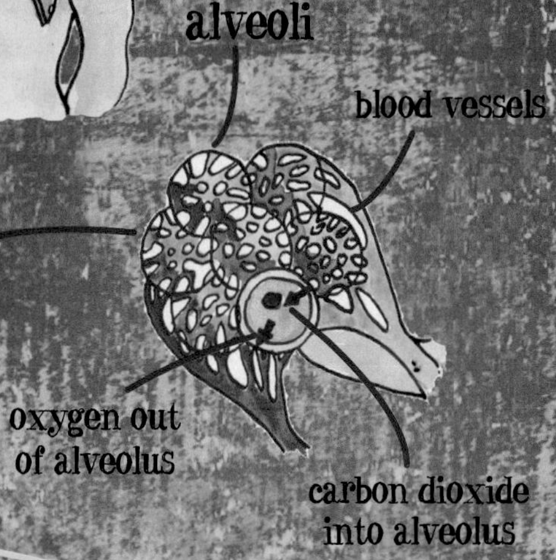

alveoli

blood vessels

How lungs work

oxygen out
of alveolus

carbon dioxide
into alveolus

Lungs and breathing

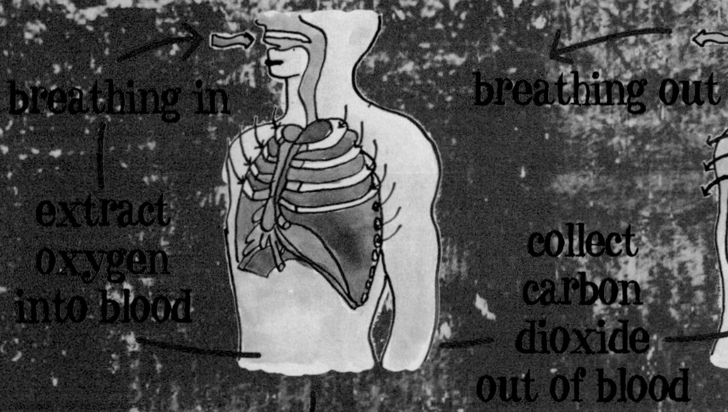

Lung parts

Breathing tubes

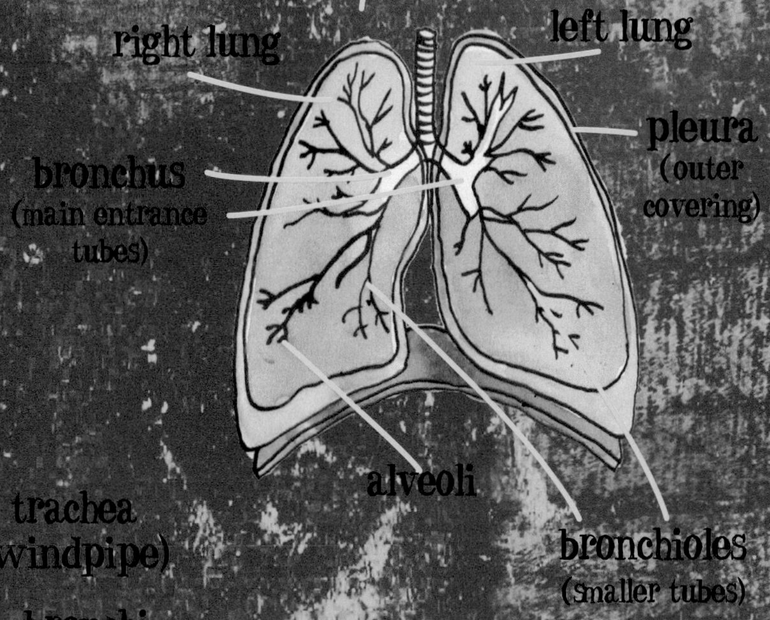

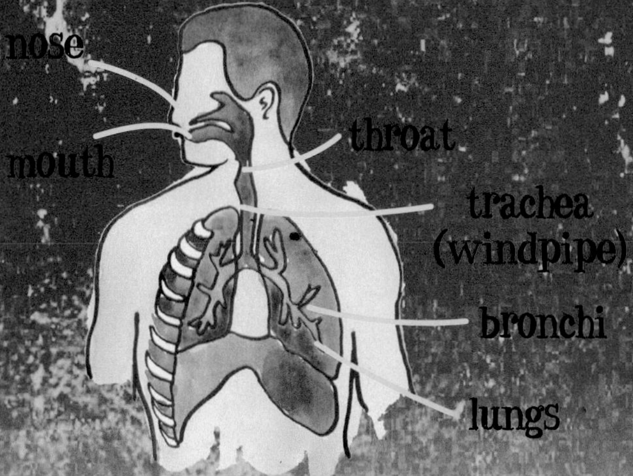

right lung

left lung

pleura
(outer
covering)

bronchus
(main entrance
tubes)

nose

mouth

throat

trachea
(windpipe)

bronchi

lungs

alveoli

bronchioles
(smaller tubes)

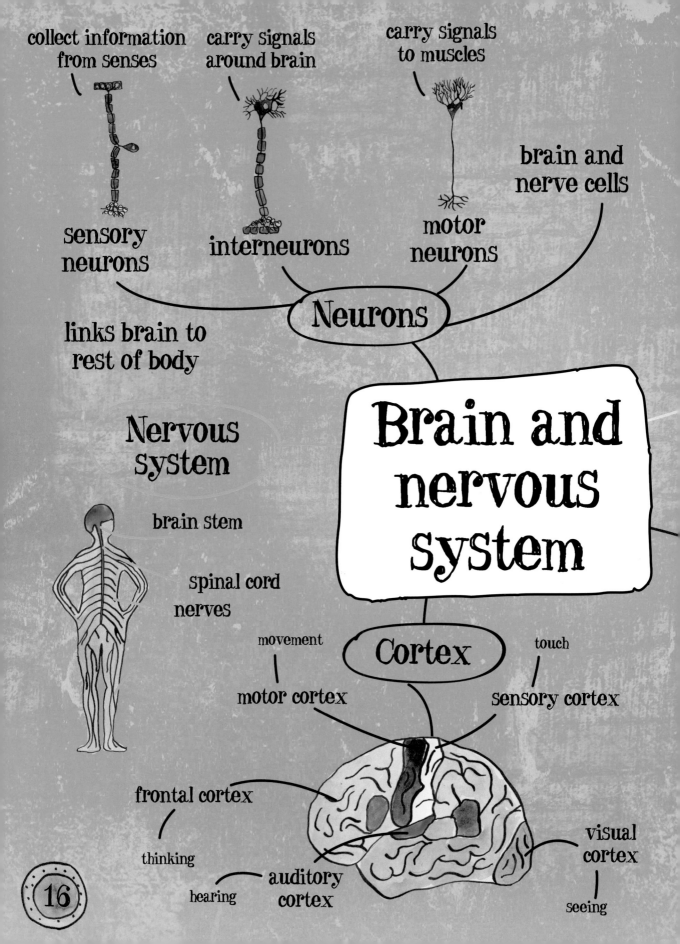

collect information
from senses

carry signals
around brain

carry signals
to muscles

brain and
nerve cells

sensory
neurons

interneurons

motor
neurons

Neurons

links brain to
rest of body

Nervous
system

brain stem

spinal cord
nerves

movement

touch

Cortex

motor cortex

sensory cortex

frontal cortex

visual
cortex

thinking

auditory
cortex

hearing

seeing

Brain and
nervous
system

16

thinking and understanding

making decisions

controlling the body

taking in information

Brain jobs

learning

storing and remembering memories

Brain parts

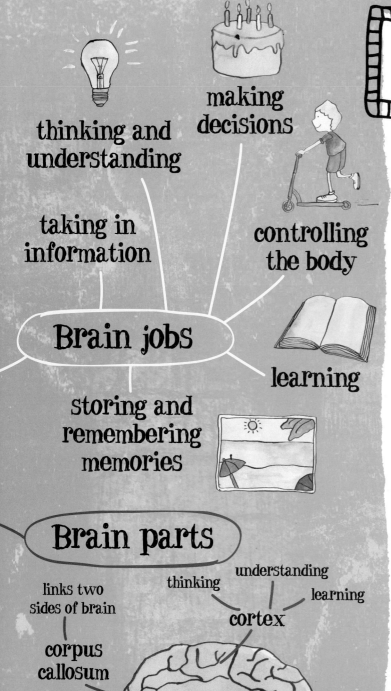

links two sides of brain

thinking

understanding

learning

cortex

corpus callosum

emotions

limbic system

memory

brain stem

cerebellum

controls basic functions

leads to body

movement

balance

The brain is the control centre of your whole body. It is in charge of taking in information, deciding what to do and making it happen. It also controls a lot of other things that you don't think about, like keeping your heart beating, making you grow and breathing while you're asleep.

Your brain fills up most of your head and looks like a wobbly, wrinkly, greyish-pink jelly. It has several main parts, including the limbic system in the middle, which deals with emotions and memories, the cerebellum at the back, which controls movement, and the cortex, the brain's covering, which is where thinking happens.

Network of nerves

The cortex is made up of a huge tangle of tree-like brain cells, or neurons, that pass signals to each other. More neurons make up the nervous system, a network of pathways called nerves that connect the brain to the rest of the body. They collect information from the senses and take it to the brain. They also carry instructions from the brain to the muscles to control everything you do.

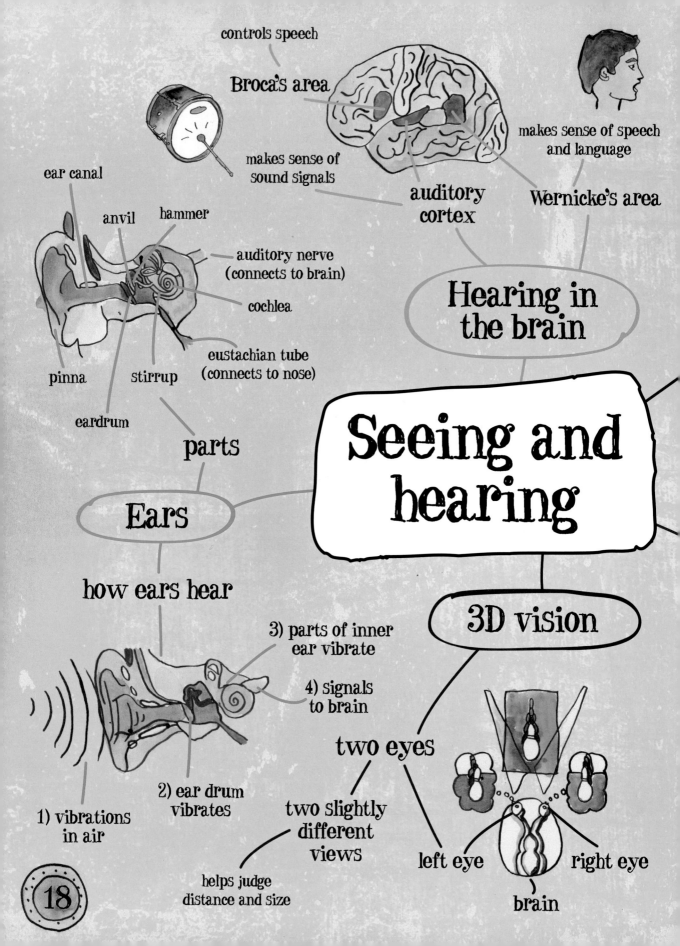

Seeing and hearing

controls speech

Broca's area

makes sense of
sound signals

**auditory
cortex**

makes sense of speech
and language

Wernicke's area

Hearing in the brain

ear canal

anvil

hammer

auditory nerve
(connects to brain)

cochlea

pinna

stirrup

eardrum

eustachian tube
(connects to nose)

parts

Ears

how ears hear

3) parts of inner
ear vibrate

4) signals
to brain

2) ear drum
vibrates

1) vibrations
in air

3D vision

two eyes

two slightly
different
views

helps judge
distance and size

left eye

right eye

brain

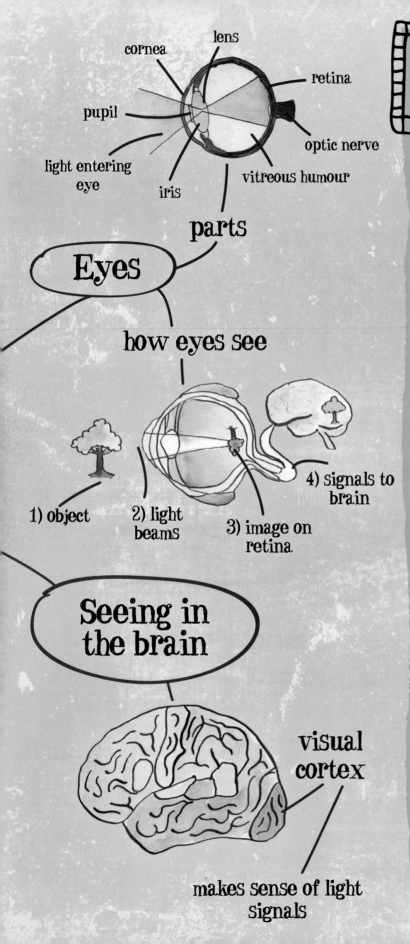

cornea
lens
retina
pupil
optic nerve
light entering eye
iris
vitreous humour

parts

Eyes

how eyes see

1) object
2) light beams
3) image on retina
4) signals to brain

Seeing in the brain

visual cortex

makes sense of light signals

When you see, your eyes are collecting patterns of light from your surroundings. Light glows from light sources like lamps or the Sun, and also bounces off other objects. From here, beams of light enter your eyes. Each eye focuses the light beams onto the retina at the back of the eyeball, where they trigger light-detecting rod and cone cells. They send signals along nerves leading into the brain, where you make sense of the patterns you can see.

Hearing

Sounds happen when objects move or vibrate, setting up sound vibrations that spread out into the air. These vibrations make parts inside your ears vibrate too, and this is how you detect sounds. Deep inside each ear, the vibrations are detected by tiny hairs connected to nerves leading to the brain. The brain works out what you can hear, based on the speed and strength of the vibrations.

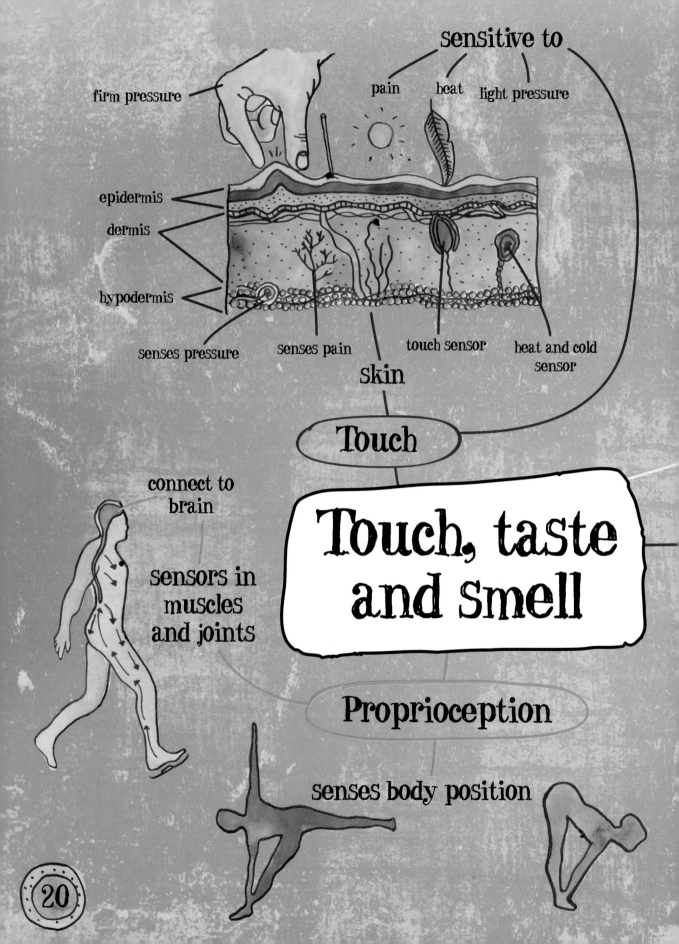

firm pressure

sensitive to

pain heat light pressure

epidermis

dermis

hypodermis

senses pressure senses pain touch sensor heat and cold sensor

Skin

Touch

connect to brain

sensors in muscles and joints

Touch, taste and Smell

Proprioception

senses body position

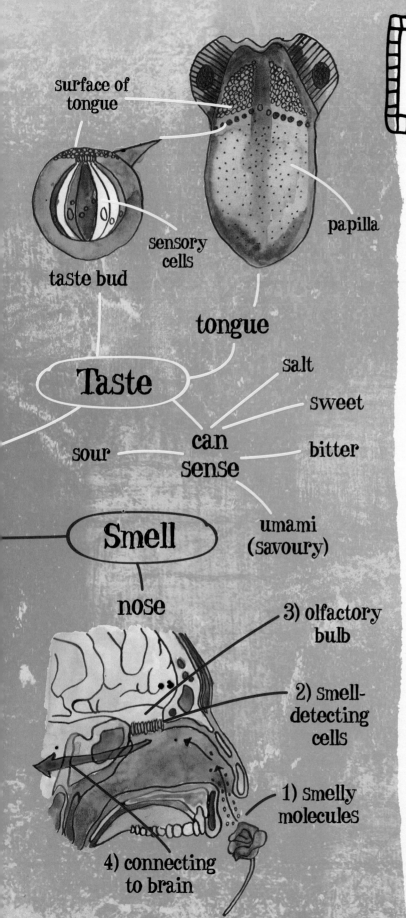

surface of
tongue

papilla

sensory
cells

taste bud

tongue

Taste

salt

sweet

sour

can
sense

bitter

Smell

umami
(savoury)

nose

3) olfactory
bulb

2) smell-
detecting
cells

1) smelly
molecules

4) connecting
to brain

Touch, taste and Smell

Smell

You smell things when molecules (tiny parts) of them float into the air and up your nose. They touch an area of smell-detecting cells inside the top of your nose, and trigger some of them. The smell signals go to your brain to tell you what you can smell – stinky socks, burnt toast or spring flowers.

Taste

You taste food when it touches your tongue and dissolves. The dissolved food flows into gaps in your tongue and touches tiny taste-sensing organs called taste buds. However, to taste things properly, you also use your sense of smell at the same time.

Touch

Your skin contains millions of nerves that can detect different kinds of touch sensation – light pressure, firm pressure, pain, heat and cold. There are also touch sensors inside your body that tell you the position your body is in. This touch sense is called proprioception.

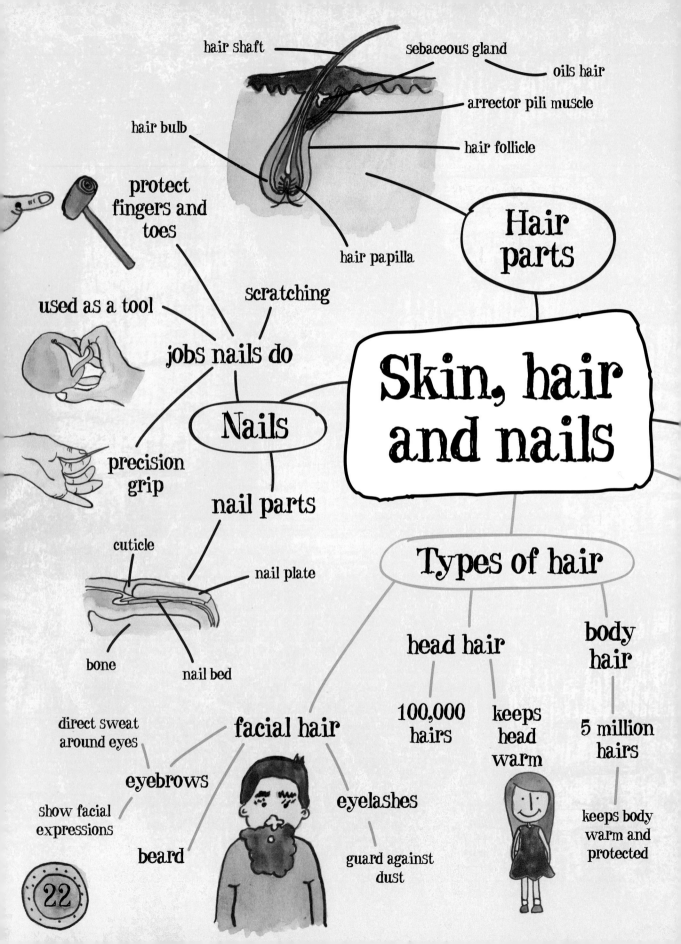

hair shaft

sebaceous gland

oils hair

arrector pili muscle

hair bulb

hair follicle

protect fingers and toes

hair papilla

Hair parts

scratching

used as a tool

jobs nails do

Skin, hair and nails

precision grip

Nails

nail parts

cuticle

Types of hair

nail plate

bone

nail bed

head hair

body hair

direct sweat around eyes

facial hair

100,000 hairs

keeps head warm

5 million hairs

eyebrows

show facial expressions

eyelashes

beard

guard against dust

keeps body warm and protected

Skin, hair and nails

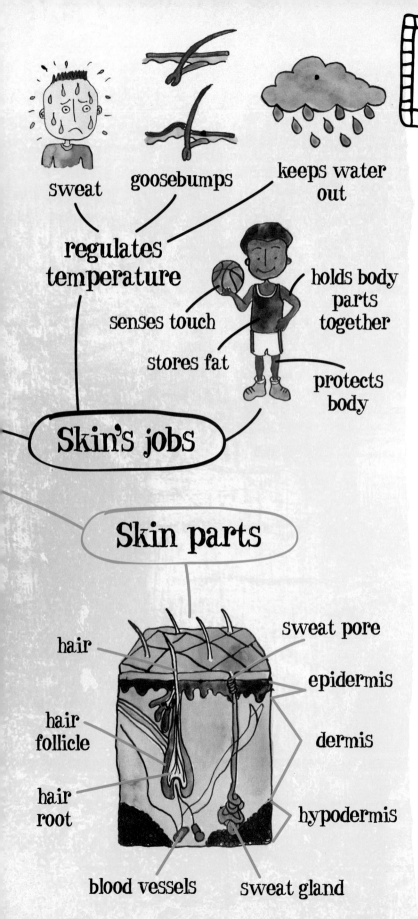

sweat

goosebumps

keeps water out

regulates temperature

senses touch

holds body parts together

stores fat

protects body

Skin's jobs

Skin parts

hair

hair follicle

hair root

sweat pore

epidermis

dermis

hypodermis

blood vessels   sweat gland

Your skin is one of the biggest body parts you have. It's a thick, protective covering, made up of several layers, that reaches all over and around you. Skin does several jobs. It holds all your body parts, organs, blood and blood vessels together, keeping them safely enclosed. It stops the body from drying out. but also stops water getting in when you're in the bath.

Skin contains touch-sensitive nerves (see page 20), allowing you to feel things all over your body. It releases chemicals that help to kill germs. Lastly, skin helps to keep your body at the right temperature. It releases sweat to help you cool down, and gives you goosebumps to help you warm up.

Hair and nails

Your skin is alive, except for a layer of dead cells on the surface. Nails and hair are also made of dead cells. They grow as more and more cells are gradually pushed out of your skin. Because they are dead, it doesn't hurt when you trim them!

Digestive system

The digestive system is the body system that takes in food and breaks it down so the body can use it. It's a long passageway, made up of several connected tubes and organs, that runs right through your body. Food starts off being chewed in your mouth, then swallowed. It passes down the oesophagus into the stomach, where it gets mushed up into liquid. Then it flows through the small intestine, where food chemicals are soaked up into the blood. Finally, the leftovers enter the large intestine, where they collect into lumps of waste, or faeces (poo).

Extra organs

The digestive system also includes the liver, gall bladder and pancreas. They release body substances that flow into the intestines to help digest food.

Waste water

Your body also has two kidneys that collect waste chemicals and liquid from your blood. This liquid waste is called urine, or wee. It is stored in the bladder and leaves the body through a tube called the urethra.

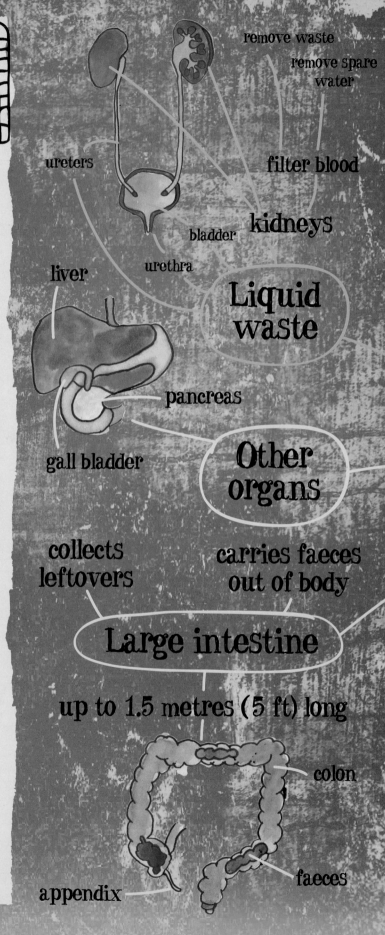

remove waste

remove spare water

filter blood

ureters

kidneys

bladder

urethra

liver

Liquid waste

pancreas

Other organs

gall bladder

collects leftovers

carries faeces out of body

Large intestine

up to 1.5 metres (5 ft) long

colon

appendix

faeces

Digestive system

Chewing and swallowing

molars
chew/grind food

canines
grip and cut food

teeth

tongue

saliva
(spit)

throat

swallow food

to stomach

oesophagus

incisors
bite food

TONGUE

Stomach

fundus
(top end)

pylorus
(bottom end)

muscles
squeeze
food

liquid

Small intestine

up to 6 metres
(20 ft) long

lined with villi

villi

small intestines

circular folds

pass into blood

soak up food
chemicals

25

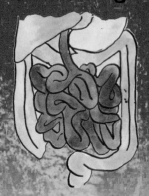

Healthy eating

Food is the body's fuel. It gives all our cells the energy they need to work, so that they can do things like making muscles move, sending signals to and from the brain or attacking germs. Our bodies also use chemicals from food to grow, repair injuries and make body substances. We have to eat a balanced diet, containing a wide range of different foods, to get all the chemicals the body needs.

Types of food

There are several main types of food that do different jobs in the body. Carbohydrates, including sugar, provide energy. Proteins help us build and repair body parts. Fats contain energy and also help to protect organs, fight diseases and make nerves work. The body also needs small amounts of vitamins, minerals and trace elements, such as iron, zinc and Vitamin C.

Water

All the body's cells need water to work, and it's also an important part of blood, sweat, and saliva. We need plenty of water (or drinks that are mostly made of water) every day.

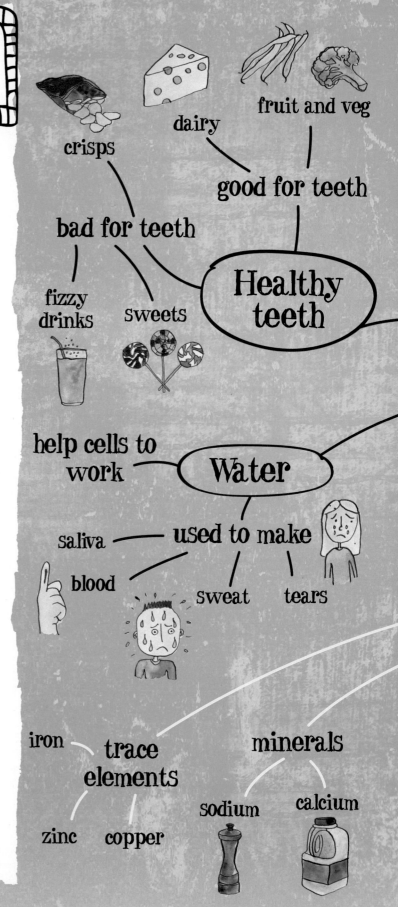

crisps

dairy

fruit and veg

good for teeth

bad for teeth

Healthy teeth

fizzy drinks

sweets

help cells to work

Water

saliva

used to make

blood

sweat

tears

iron

trace elements

minerals

zinc

copper

sodium

calcium

repairing
body

building body
parts

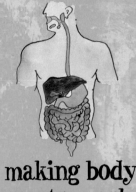

making body
parts work

energy

What is food for?

Healthy eating

pasta   sugars

cereal

bread

carbohydrates

Types of food

eggs

vitamins

potatoes

fat

butter

protein

citrus fruit

oils

nuts

cheese

meat

fish

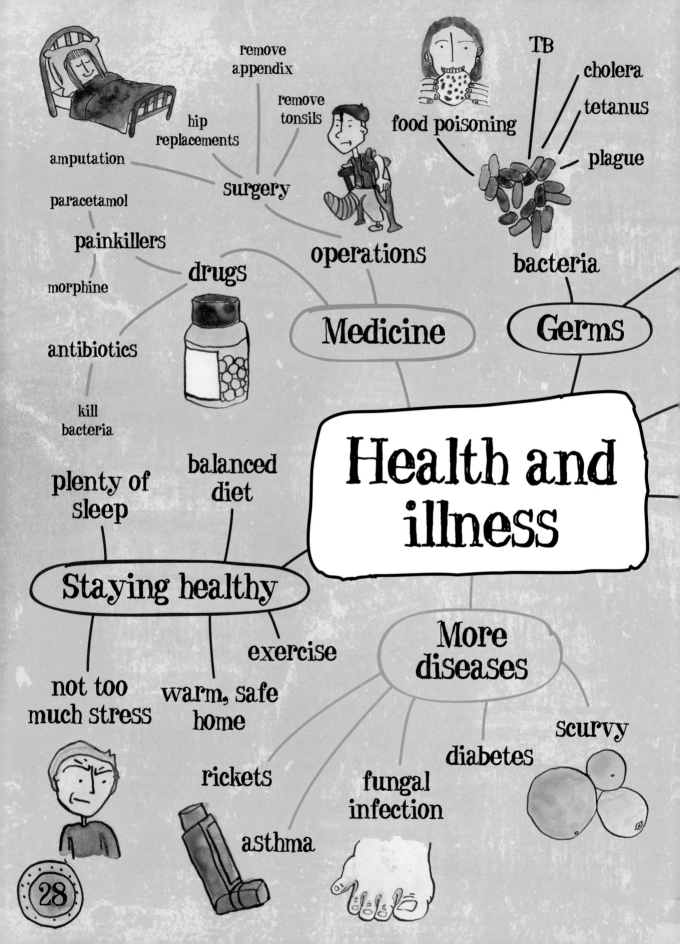

remove appendix

hip replacements

remove tonsils

food poisoning

TB

cholera

tetanus

plague

amputation

surgery

operations

bacteria

paracetamol

painkillers

drugs

Medicine

Germs

morphine

antibiotics

kill bacteria

Health and illness

plenty of sleep

balanced diet

Staying healthy

More diseases

exercise

scurvy

not too much stress

warm, safe home

diabetes

rickets

fungal infection

asthma

28

Health and illness

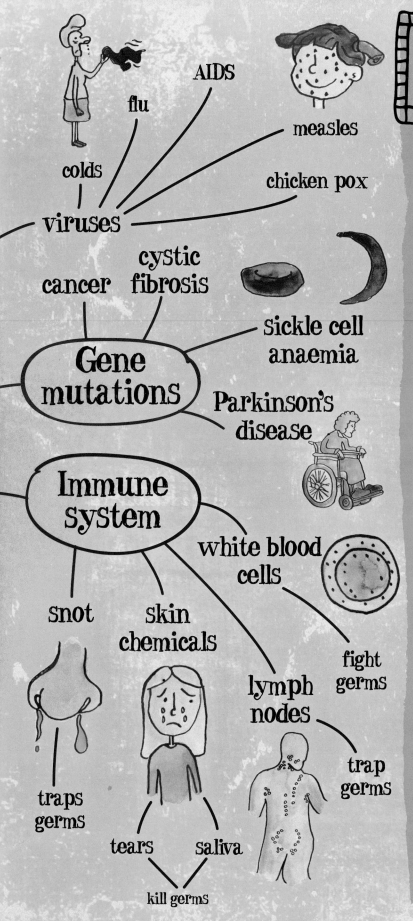

AIDS

flu

colds

measles

chicken pox

viruses

cancer

cystic fibrosis

Gene mutations

Sickle cell anaemia

Parkinson's disease

Immune system

white blood cells

snot

Skin chemicals

fight germs

lymph nodes

traps germs

trap germs

tears

saliva

kill germs

A healthy human body is one that has nothing wrong with it and is working well. But the body can go wrong and become ill or sick. Some illnesses are caused by germs getting into the body. For example, bacteria such as Salmonella can cause food poisoning, and colds are caused by tiny germs called viruses. Other germs cause diseases like malaria, tuberculosis (TB) and measles.

Some diseases, such as cystic fibrosis and some types of cancer, are caused by mutations or problems in a person's genes. Some are caused by an unhealthy lifestyle or surroundings – for example, a lack of sunlight can give you rickets, and not enough Vitamin C causes scurvy.

Fighting disease
A body system called the immune system fights germs and diseases. It includes white blood cells that attack germs, and chemicals in tears, saliva and stomach acid that kill germs.

Glossary

alveoli Tiny chambers in the lungs that extract oxygen from the air.

arteries Blood vessels that lead away from the heart.

bacteria Germs that can cause some types of diseases.

blood vessels Tubes that carry blood around the body.

body system Group of organs and body parts that work together to do a job in the body.

bone marrow Soft substance found inside some bones.

carbohydrate A type of food that gives the body energy.

cardiac muscle A type of muscle found in the heart.

cell membrane Outer covering or skin of a cell.

cells Very small units that living things are made up of.

cerebellum Area at the back of the brain, used to control movement and balance.

compact bone Hard, solid type of bone.

cortex Wrinkled covering of the brain, used for thinking and understanding.

cytoplasm Jelly-like fluid inside a cell.

faeces Poo.

gall bladder Small organ that stores chemicals that help the body digest food.

genes Instructions found inside the nucleus of cells that control how cells work.

hormones Chemicals used by the body to send signals between body parts.

intestines Tubes that soak up chemicals from food and collect unwanted waste.

kidneys Two organs that filter the blood and remove waste chemicals and spare water.

limbic system Part of the brain that deals with emotions and memories.

liver Large organ that helps to digest food and stores useful chemicals.

minerals Non-living substances such as calcium that the body needs in order to work.

nerves Pathways that carry signals between the brain and the body.

neurons Cells that make up the brain and nerves.

nucleus The control centre of a cell.

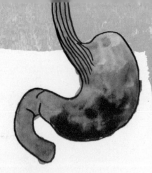

oesophagus Tube leading from the throat into the stomach.

organelles Tiny organ-like parts inside cells.

organs Body parts that do a particular job, such as the brain and stomach.

oxygen Gas found in the air that cells need in order to work.

pancreas Small organ that helps the body digest food.

periosteum Tough outer covering of a bone.

proprioception Sense of where the body is and the position it is in.

protein A type of food the body uses to grow, make body substances and repair injuries.

retina Layer at the back of the eyeball that senses light.

skeletal muscles Muscles that are attached to bones and make them move.

smooth muscle A type of muscle found in body organs and tissues.

spongy bone Light, honeycomb-like bone found inside some bones.

taste buds Tiny taste-sensing organs found in the tongue.

tendon Strong, stretchy cord that attaches a muscle to a bone.

trace elements Substances in food that the body needs tiny amounts of.

trachea Tube leading from the throat to the lungs.

urethra Tube that carries urine (wee) from the bladder out of the body.

urine Wee.

veins Blood vessels that lead towards the heart.

virus Tiny germ that can cause some types of diseases.

vitamins Chemicals that the body needs small amounts of in order to work.

windpipe Another name for the trachea.

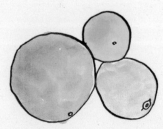

Index